BUILD TO WIN

A PLAYBOOK FOR ENTREPRENEURIAL SUCCESS

Marvin E. Carolina, Jr.

No part of this publication may be reproduced or transmitted in any form or by any means, mechanical or electronic, including photocopying for recording, or by any information storage and retrieval system, without express written permission from the publisher.

Copyright © 2017 Marvin Carolina, Jr.

All rights reserved.

ISBN-13:978-0997878615

ISBN-10:0997878614

Printed in the U.S.A.

First Edition

BUILD TO WIN

A PLAYBOOK FOR ENTREPRENEURIAL SUCCESS

Marvin E. Carolina, Jr.

Build to Win

TABLE OF CONTENTS

Acknowledgements		vii
Introduction		ix

Chapter 1	The Best Way to Win Business	11
Chapter 2	What Is In It For Me?	15
Chapter 3	Where Is Your Business Headed?	19
Chapter 4	More Than A Degree and Good Grades	23
Chapter 5	What Motivates You?	27
Chapter 6	Business by Numbers	31
Chapter 7	Who is Your Customer?	37
Chapter 8	How Has Your Journey Been?	43
Chapter 9	Easy Math: Path to Profit	47
Chapter 10	Are You Moving Too Fast?	51
Chapter 11	You Are in a Race!	57
Chapter 12	Insurance Is the Biggest Waste of Money… Until You Need It!	63
Chapter 13	Job Well Done	67
Chapter 14	Social Skills: Still on Top	71
Chapter 15	Stand Out in a Crowded Market	75
Chapter 16	Strategies vs. Tactics	79
Chapter 17	This Is Not Working	83
Chapter 18	Who Monitors Your Technology?	89
Chapter 19	Hire A Business Consultant … For Free	93
Chapter 20	Failing In Good Times	99
Chapter 21	The Tired Entrepreneur	103

Conclusion		107
About the Author		109

Marvin Carolina Jr.

ACKNOWLEDGEMENTS

This is my second book after a very successful and strong reception to the first book. My goal and focus is to continue to help people live their dreams.

I want to again thank my fabulous wife Michelle, who has been with me every step of this journey and we have enjoyed every step together.

My team continues to be awesome as we continue our mission. Thank you, thank you, thank you. I cannot thank you all enough:

- Dr. Amanda Goodson (Dr. G), your guidance, mentorship and prayers continue to motivate and inspire me.
- Edward Cates, your ability to reach more and more people with our message continues to amaze me
- Ed Long, your talent to dot the I's and cross the T's makes our message clear and direct.

Marvin Carolina Jr.

INTRODUCTION

Having the ability to compete in today's business environment is a key to success, as well as, understanding the rules of competition and the impact. Sometimes competition is viewed as negative, but we compete every day. Some people just do it a lot better than others.

I continue to see people succeed and fail in business, all types of people from different backgrounds, religions, socioeconomic levels, age, culture and gender. Most of the time it is because they do not have enough information and have not implemented the correct strategy. This book is designed to give information in which you can develop a winning strategy.

I want people to live their dreams of entrepreneurship and business owner, as well as, be successful. Competition is a huge part of being successful in business and in life. Compiled in this book are several best practices and suggestions that will help you successfully move forward. The chapters are short, direct and a quick read. They are designed to make you smile and laugh Most of all it is designed to make you think about the way you are currently doing things and what changes you should implement. My goal is for you to read the book and make some positive changes, then tell me the impact it has made on your life.

Marvin Carolina Jr.

Chapter 1

The Best Way to Win Business

There are lots of ways to increase your odds of winning a prospect's business—asking what they need and why they need it, conducting powerful PowerPoint presentations, emphasizing the benefits your product or service provides, listening more than talking—but experience has taught me that what gives you the best chance of winning business is being prepared.

Being prepared means that even before you walk into the meeting with your prospect you have envisioned the meeting in your mind. You have gone over every question you may be asked and have rehearsed your responses *at least* several times. Here are a few questions your prospect may ask you:

- Do you use your product or service?
- How can I justify the price of your product or service?
- What are my options if I change my mind?

- What recent changes have you made to your product or service?
- Who is your ideal customer?
- Who (specifically) will manage my account if I give you my business?
- Why are you more/less expensive than your competitors?

Props

Answering all of your prospect's questions to their satisfaction increases your chances of winning their business, but even the most-convincing responses can only do so much. Responses appeal to their intellect; props appeal to their emotions. If you can create the right emotional response in your prospect, you are much more likely to get their business. How do you do that?

Your competitors will likely be armed with props when they visit prospects too, but you set yourself apart by having props specifically designed for your prospect. Assume a photographer was trying to win your business and they showed you their portfolio full of award-winning pictures. Now assume they showed you pictures of your business that they had taken, showing your business from a number of angles each more impressive than the one before. Which set of pictures would create the greater emotional response?

Is It Easy?

Some prospects are hesitant to do business with you, because they assume they will have to do extra work. Staying with the photographer, how would you feel if they told you they would be happy to take as many pictures of you as you like—all you have to do is come to their studio across town?

Your goal as a small-business owner is to meet the needs of your clients, but you should not disrupt their schedules doing it. Make it convenient for them to do business with you. If the photographer said they would come to your office or any other place you suggested and take the pictures, you would be *much* more likely to do business with them.

No Surprises

I know people who have gone into sales meetings having done little or no research on their prospects. They were confident in their abilities, because they knew their products and services inside-out, but more importantly, they considered themselves quick on their feet. I was guilty of using this approach until I began noticing a pattern: A prospect would ask questions about their business or their market that I could not answer, I promised I would follow-up, and when I did, they were no longer interested.

Expect questions about your prospect and their business! After all, that is what is most important to them. Read about them and their business, but also talk to people who know them and know their business needs. If you have researched your prospect *and* their business, you will be able to answer 90% of their questions and the 10% you cannot answer will not offer major surprises.

My Experience

When I launched my beverage business in Atlanta, I sold bottled water; as sales grew, I added bottled juice. I pitched my juice to each client, answering their questions and refuting their objections, but instead of waiting for them to decide, I told them I had juice on the truck and that I would leave a case with them to see if their customers wanted it—I added that juice bottles have already been priced. Having juice on-hand and already priced persuaded client-after-client to begin giving me their juice business.

Conclusion

Whether it is a question the prospect wants answered or a prop they want to see, be prepared. If you are not and are forced to follow-up, you give competitors an opportunity to win their business in the interim, and you also give prospects time to lose interest. Being prepared means you not only know your business inside-out—you know *their* business inside-out.

Chapter 2

What Is In It for Me?

When I owned my business in Atlanta, selling bottled water and bottled juice, one of the ways I differentiated my service from the competition was by doing little things that helped my customers. For example, when I delivered my beverages, instead of simply stacking them on the floor in the stockroom—like my competitors did—I cut the tops off of my boxes so the employees could easily get to my beverages. I also put price tags on all of my beverages. My customers told me they appreciated my doing this, and more importantly, they rewarded me by remaining loyal customers.

I obviously didn't have to do this for my customers, but I knew they would notice it and I knew they would value it. If I hadn't spent 30 to 45 minutes opening my boxes and pricing my beverages, my clients' employees would have had to do it, so I was providing the employees 30 to 45 additional minutes to spend on other tasks. I was also providing a valuable, time-saving service that prospective customers would value, so whenever I pitched someone, I told them I did more than just drop off their beverages.

Great salespeople don't go on-and-on about what their product or service can do (describing features): They go on-and-on about what their product or service can do *for you* (describing benefits). When I met with prospective customers, I explained my drop-off process, but I spent most of my time talking about how my process would help their business.

Features Vs. Benefits

There is an easy way to tell the difference between a feature and a benefit: When discussing a feature, the focus is on your product or service, but when discussing a benefit, the focus is on your customer. Features are important—and more than a few prospective customers were impressed when I told them that I delivered *and* prepped my product—but what closed the deals was when I talked about all of the time I would save their employees.

Here is another difference between features and benefits: "Features tell, but benefits sell." No matter how wonderful your product or service is, the prospective customer only wants to know how it will help their business. So spend the majority of your time describing what it will do for them.

Listen!

Salespeople who talk a lot are rarely good at their jobs, but salespeople who listen a lot and talk little are usually good at their jobs. When meeting with a prospective customer, the most important thing you can do is listen. Don't go into the meeting thinking about all of the wonderful ways your product or service can help their business—ask questions then listen to find out what they want and what they need.

When qualifying them, think about how your product or service can deliver what they want or what they need; and when it's your time to respond, mention the features you offer, but talk at-length about the benefits you will provide.

Explain

It is perfectly fine to tell prospective customers that you use the most innovative technology in the industry, for example, provided you also tell them that using your technology equips them to do business with small businesses *and* large corporations, or that using your technology will reduce the time their employees spend filing documents by 50%. Always explain the benefit each feature offers. A feature by itself does not help your customer, and in most cases, the customer does not understand them.

When you explain the benefit; however, the customer understands because you are describing things they understand and value, such as, higher quality, increased efficiency or productivity, lower cost, and time saved. Do not assume your customer or prospective customer will identify every benefit each of your features offers: Point them out!

Conclusion

When talking about your business, sell benefits. Features are nice, but people want to know what those fancy features will do for them. Take inventory of your business and find every feature it offers, and for each of them—no matter how small or seemingly unimportant—figure out what benefit it offers; so when you are talking to a prospective customer, you will know exactly what your business can do for them.

Chapter 3

Where Is Your Business Headed?

In his bestseller *7 Habits of Highly Effective People*, *Stephen Covey says* highly-effective people "start with the end in mind." As a small-business owner, you should do the same: Make business decisions based on where you want your business to be in five or ten years. Ask yourself, before each decision, "Will this get me where I want to go?"

The first thing you should do is visualize how you want your business to look in the future. It does not matter how much or how little time you invest in this exercise. It can be 30 minutes, but be specific! Saying your goal is to make $500,000 in annual sales is specific. Saying your goal is to make a lot of money is not. Remember: Your business is yours, so you can make it look any way you want.

In order to grow your business and realize its potential, you have to consistently make good decisions. I have met far too many small-business owners who have admitted they are in the habit of making decisions that will get them to the next month. Practicing this short-sighted—yet popular—approach to decision-making will almost ensure you will not arrive where you intended.

Why *are* you in business? To make money? This is not a good reason to be in business, because you can make money lots of ways. If providing the best product or service is not your primary reason for being in business, your competitors—who *are* trying to provide the best product or service—will eventually snatch your market share and drive you out of the market.

How do you work backwards? With goals. Elbert Hubbard, an American philanthropist, said it well: "Many people fail in life, not for lack of ability or brains or even courage but simply because they have never organized their energies around a goal."

Highly-effective people set goals. As a small-business owner, you should not only set goals, you should also communicate them to your employees. I recommend using SMART goals. There are variations on the *SMART* acronym, and those variations are similar, but I prefer each business goal be the following:

Specific: The more specific your goal, the better.
Measurable: Have tangible criteria for measuring progress.

Assignable: Decide who will accomplish what, and let them know.

Realistic: You must be willing *and* able to accomplish each goal given your resources and time.

Time-Sensitive: With no time-limit, there is no urgency.

There are lots of paths you can take in business, and with each decision, you either keep your business on the path you want or take it down another. Like driving a car. When you leave home, for example, you know where you want to go, so at each intersection, you decide which street will quickly get you to your destination. Drivers know exactly where they want to go. Lots of small-business owners do not.

Marvin Carolina Jr.

Chapter 4

More Than a Degree and Good Grades

Generations ago when your grandparents were looking for work, a high-school diploma would impress a prospective employer. A generation ago, a college degree. If you want to impress a prospective employer in today's ultracompetitive job market, a college degree by itself will not do—even with excellent grades.

Distinguish Yourself

Hundreds of applicants will be applying for the jobs you will be applying for, so your credentials will have to stand out. Your degree and grade-point-average may get the Human Resource Representative's attention, but what will they see on your resume that persuades them to call you for an interview?

Leadership on a sports team or in a campus organization? A major perfectly-suited for the job? Involvement in extracurricular activities?

Employers look favorably on each of these, but if you want the HR Representative to put your resume in their for-further-consideration pile, you need what they crave: work experience.

The Right Experience

The National Association of Colleges and Employers (NACE) conducted a study in 2014 and found that while grade-point-average is important, it is not the most important consideration. While 68% of employers screen candidates by grade-point-average, even more screen candidates based on the following: ability to work as part of a team (77%), leadership (77%), written communication skills (73%), problem-solving skills (70%), strong work ethic (70%).

By comparison, more than 90% of them cited a preference to hire college graduates with work experience! It was not just any work experience. If you held a job in high school or college that was not similar to the professional job you hope to land, that experience will likely be ignored. Only 20% of employers prefer to hire candidates with *any* type of work experience, while

72% prefer candidates with relevant work experience; thus, the kind an internship provides.

The Wrong Career

It is not uncommon for a college student to get the job of their dreams only to discover it is not the job for them. No matter how much you learn about your industry—from professors, from textbooks, online, or by word-of-mouth—there is no substitute for first-hand experience.

You may have convinced yourself you will thrive in a fast-paced environment, but unless you have worked in a fast-paced environment, you cannot be sure. Seeing your job or your industry up-close allows you to determine if you have what it takes to do the job and to determine if you actually like the job.

If you are not sure what job you want or what industry you want to work in, accepting internships in different fields will help you decide what feels right and what does not.

Conclusion

Employers are demanding more from employees than ever; employers are also demanding more from college graduates. College students have taken notice: according to the 2014 study, of the Class of 2015 graduates who earned their Bachelor's degree, 65% of them participated in an internship program. The highest percentage recorded.

Times have changed, and to have any chance of distinguishing yourself in a deluge of job seekers, you need more than a degree and good grades. An internship impresses the HR Representative while also teaching you about your industry and about yourself.

Chapter 5

What Motivates You?

I've spent the last ten years teaching small-business owners across the country how to make their businesses more profitable, and one of the things I like to find out is, what motivated them to start their businesses. These are the reasons they gave:

- Bored with their jobs
- Didn't like answering to anyone
- No future for them where they were working
- Not making enough money where they were working
- Thought they could do a better job than their bosses were doing
- To get rich
- To pursue their passion
- Underemployed
- Unemployed
- Wanted something to pass down to their children

- Wanted to control their destinies
- Wanted to employ people in their communities
- Wanted to train young people in their communities

Why did you start *your* business? Whether you've been in business one year or twenty years, what were your reasons for starting your business? If you didn't plan to become a small-business owner—if you just fell into it—that's fine too. Some of the participants in my classes have said they're surprised they're in business because being a business owner was never a goal of theirs. How could that happen? Consider this.

People always told you, you were an excellent cook, and for whatever reason, you began cooking and selling Sunday dinners. You sold most of them to family, friends, and neighbors, but as the demand for your dinners increased, people you didn't know began buying them.

As you counted how much money you'd made each Sunday, you realized you made more on Sunday than you made for the entire week at your *real* job. In addition, you love to cook. So you decide to open your restaurant.

What About Now?

No matter what your reasons for going into business, ask yourself this: Are those reasons still valid? If one of your reasons was, you had a passion for producing your product or service, do you *still* have that passion? Perhaps you were so passionate you told yourself if you ever start your own business, you'd wake-up at 5:00 every morning and work twelve-hour days.

Now that you've been in business awhile, are you still that passionate—or are you waking-up at 9:00 every morning and working six-hour days? If this or something similar describes you but you're pleased with how your business is performing, then that's fine. I'm not judging. I simply want you to compare your motivation now with your motivation then.

Whether you call it ambition, drive, passion, or desperation, do you still have it? If so, do you have as much as you had when you started your business?

Changes Along the Way

As you reflect on your reasons for starting your business, you may want to revise some of those reasons. Say, for example, one of your goals was to get rich. Even though you earn a healthy business salary—more than you ever made as an employee—you realize your business salary won't make you rich.

You would probably be wise to amend this reason because if you don't, and you fail to become rich, it might disappoint you. When in fact you should celebrate how well you've done in business and realize you'll make more than you would have made as an employee.

Looking Back

As you reflect on your business journey, was it different than expected? If so, how was it different? What information is available to you now that wasn't available to you when you started your business (or what information are you aware of now that you weren't aware of when you started)?

Business, like life, teaches valuable lessons, but you shouldn't keep those lessons to yourself. Share them! You can help other small-business owners—some who started their businesses for the same reasons you started yours—avoid some of the mistakes you made.

Conclusion

In talking to hundreds of small-business owners over the years, I've identified one thing that is most-responsible for the quality of their product or service. Desire. If you still desire doing what you love, you'll produce a good product or service. If you still desire to provide employment to the people in your community, you'll produce a good product or service. On the other hand, if your desire has waned, the quality of what you produce will also wane.

Your reasons for being in business may be different than when you started, and if so, that's fine. Just be sure you know what those reasons are.

Chapter 6

Business By Numbers

"I shall try not to use statistics as a drunken man uses lamp-posts, for support rather than for illumination." (Andrew Lang, Scottish novelist)

How is business? When I ask that question, I usually have an ulterior motive. I ask to gauge how well you know your business. Most small business owners do not know how their business is doing. When they say, "Business is great. Sales are up," I think to myself, "A business can lose money when sales are up." If you are not tracking the numbers, you do not *know* how your business is doing.

According to a 2014 survey of 1200 small business owners, 79% of them said they use numbers to inform them of their business decisions. Why? Because 75% of them believe using numbers gives them a competitive advantage.

To ensure your business is the best it can be, in a competitive, crowded marketplace, you *must* track and use the numbers. Track what works and what does not, and let that information drive your business decisions. Here is an example:

Assume you are a Real Estate Agent. You have been a successful Agent for years, and finding leads going door-to-door has worked well for as long as you can remember, but younger Agents are finding more leads and making more money than you and they are not working as hard as you!

Had you tracked the numbers, you would have known door-to-door prospecting is no longer efficient. The younger Agents may not be working as hard as you, but they are working more efficiently than you by prospecting on Facebook, LinkedIn, and Twitter. They are reaching more prospective customers in a day—sitting at their desks—than you are reaching in a week going door-to-door.

Who Is Your Customer?

I cannot emphasize this enough: *Know your customer base.* According to the 80/20 Rule, formally known as the Pareto Principle, without knowing anything about your business, I can say this with confidence: 20% of your customers account for 80% of your sales. This 20% is your customer base.

By tracking customer demographics, you know who your customer is. Also, by making your business decisions with your customer in mind, you are running your business at peak efficiency. Assume your customer, the 20% who generate 80% of your sales, is 55- to 70-years-old. Would it make business sense to expend 50% of your marketing efforts on 18- to 24-year-olds? Of course not. Nor would it make business sense to market to everyone when it is obvious *your* customer is between 55 and 70.

The more customer data you track—age, education, ethnicity, gender, geographic location, income, marital status, race—the more specific your customer. Do not just track the information. Use it! According to the 2014 survey, 52% of small business owners use data to determine where to market.

Equipment Too

In addition to tracking customers, you also want to track inventory and equipment. Assume you own a trucking company and have four trucks. You need to track how much money each truck makes, but you also need to track their expenses:

- Fuel
- Insurance
- Labor
- Maintenance
- Miscellaneous expenses (e.g., tires)

- Tax (business, property)

By studying the numbers, you discover one truck is less profitable than the other three, because the driver of the fourth truck gets fuel at a service station where fuel is 10% higher than it is at the station the other three drivers use. Had you not tracked the numbers, you would not have known.

What Numbers Should You Track?

Sales: Income from selling your product or service

Revenue: Sales plus additional income (e.g., income from investments)

Gross Profit: Sales minus direct cost (cost to produce the product or provide the service)

Net Profit (*Profit* or *Bottom Line*): Revenue minus direct cost minus indirect cost (e.g., employee benefits, salaries, taxes, miscellaneous expenses)

Your goal, as a business owner, is to increase revenue and profit. If you are tracking the numbers, you know where every dollar comes from and where every dollar goes. You *know* your business.

The Little Things

Do not overlook or fail to see the value in add-ons. Those inexpensive, seemingly-insignificant products or services that when offered, 90% of your customers agree to buy. An add-on may only make one dollar, but what if 90% of your 100 customers purchase the add-on in a week?

Where Are the Numbers?

Review these often:

Balance Sheet: Shows assets, liabilities, and equity. The balance sheet *must* balance.

Income Statement (*Profit and Loss Statement*): Shows revenue and expenses for a given period (e.g., year-to-date, month-to-date) from operating and non-operating activities.

How Does It Help?

According to the small-business owners in the 2014 survey, here is how number-tracking helped them:

- Find new customers (73%)
- Retain existing customers (67%)
- Improve customer experience (65%)

According to the small-business owners in the survey who did not track, here is why they did not:

- Do not know where to begin (49%)
- Do not have time (40%)

If you want to maintain your market share—and certainly if you want to increase it—your business *has* to be efficient. If you are not poring over the numbers and basing your decisions on them, you are giving your business a competitive *dis*-advantage. You are just winging it! So … how is business?

Chapter 7

Who is Your Customer?

Who do you want to buy your product or service? You may say "everyone," but remember this: not everyone needs or wants what you offer. So it is important you know who *does*. Knowing your customer (i.e., target market) makes your business more efficient and more profitable.

What Is A Customer?

A customer is a person or business that buys your product or service. That is obvious. I want you; however, to think of your customer as a person or business you target to buy your product or service, because your market research says they need it or want it. Everything you do, you do—or should do—with your customer in mind.

When you ask yourself this question, be honest: "Who can use my product or service?" You may *think* everyone can use your product or service, but if you examine the needs of the people or businesses in your market, you will see exactly who needs or wants what you offer.

Why Is Knowing Your Customer Important?

Assume you sell vacuum cleaners. You want to sell as many as possible, so you target small businesses, medium-size businesses, *and* large businesses. You spend $1,000 marketing to each. You are confident in your product: your vacuum cleaners are the industry's most advanced *and* most affordable. Who would not want one?

As good as they are, your vacuum cleaners are built for use in homes and small offices. Medium-size businesses and large businesses need a commercial vacuum cleaner: a larger heavy-duty machine that can be used every day on heavy-traffic carpets and will last a long time. Your vacuum cleaner simply cannot do what medium-sized businesses and large businesses need it to do.

You spent $3,000 marketing your vacuum cleaners, but $2,000 was spent on a non-existent market. Assume your marketing efforts brought ten new customers: had you spent the entire $3,000 marketing to small businesses, you would have 30 new customers, not 10.

Knowing your customer makes your business more efficient: each advertising and marketing dollar targets a person or business that needs or wants your product or service.

My Customer

I realized long ago, not every small-business owner is my customer; therefore, when I am writing my blog, I write to small-business owners with the following characteristics:

Adapts

My customer, who knows the market changes and adapts to these changes. When the market requires you to produce a better product or provide a better service—with your existing budget—do you complain and hope to get by or do you find a way ... even if it means reducing staff and relying more-heavily on technology?

When the market demands my customer change, they change, because they know resisting change makes their product, service, or way of conducting business, obsolete.

Ambitious

My customer knows what their business is capable of: they know its potential. They are willing to commit the energy, money, and time to ensure their business fulfills its potential.

Some business owners, with the same 10% of the market they had years ago, know they can double or even triple their business. They are content, though, with their market share and have no desire to work longer hours or hire staff (or additional staff). There is nothing wrong with this. Nothing at all, but this business owner is *not* my customer.

My customer knows they can corner 25% of the market and commits whatever is necessary to corner that 25%. They have one goal: realize their business' potential.

Competitive

My customer knows, no matter how good their product or service, to reach its potential, their business needs talented and well-trained employees. My customer's employees receive on-going training to keep abreast of Best Practices. Products and services evolve and so do the best ways to produce these products, as well as, offer these services.

My customer also knows there is one way to attract and retain the best talent: provide a competitive compensation package.

Courageous

Business owners who have been in business awhile fear change more than business owners who have not been in business long. Fearing change is natural, but you have a choice: change in spite of your fear, or allow your fear to trap you.

Courage is *not* being afraid: it is being afraid, but acting in spite of your fear. My customer, who has done things the same way with good results, may fear changing the way they do business, because they are not certain the change will bring better results. However, they are more afraid of this certainty: the business that resists change is not in business very long.

Cutting-Edge

My customer knows it is foolish to try to compete in today's ultra-competitive marketplace relying on IBM personal computers, for example or similarly-outdated business practices. Instead, they rely on the latest technology to manufacture their product or provide their service and Best Practices, allowing them to deliver a better product or service more efficiently.

Specializes

My customer knows, for their business to fulfill its potential, each employee has to do what they do best. If the owner has never met a computer problem they could not fix, they should fix computers all day and hire people to answer the phone, balance the ledger, vacuum the carpet, and write the marketing.

When I realized small-business owners had different goals, I made a decision: spend my energy and time helping small-business owners who want to expand operations, hire (or increase) staff, increase profit and revenue, or introduce innovative practices or technologies. In short, help them take their business to the next level.

You do not choose your customer. Your customer chooses you. In order to give them what they need and want, you have to *know* what they need and want. No matter how aggressive or well-conceived your marketing strategy, if you fail to provide what your customer needs or wants, you will fail to make them a customer.

Chapter 8

How Has Your Journey Been?

When you launched your business, embarking on a journey, what did you expect? I am not talking about the things that were in your business plan or your business goals. Reflect for a moment, and try to remember how you answered these questions:

- How do I feel about being my own boss?
- How do I feel about my industry?
- How much will I charge?
- How much money will I make?
- How will things look in six months? In a year? In five years?
- What will my business look like?
- Who will be my customers? How many customers will I have?
- Who is going to work for me?

Vision

When you think about your initial vision, have things turned out the way you envisioned? If not, are things close to how you envisioned them, or are they drastically different? Actually, the first question I should have asked is, did you even have a vision!

How Does It Compare?

I have asked you to reflect for a reason. You have been in business for five or ten years, perhaps longer or even shorter. How does the vision you have of how your business will look going forward compare to your initial vision (if you initially had one, of course)? Are the visions similar or different? If they are different, that is okay. If you did not initially have a vision, that is okay too.

Compare what you expected to experience with what you have actually experienced. Has being in business been easier or harder than expected? Has finding customers been easier or harder? What has been your most-difficult challenge? What has surprised you most? If you launched your business with no expectations—no vision—how has that served you?

What I have found is, people do not worry about what they expect to worry about? For example, before going into business, lots of people worry about having enough money to run their businesses only to discover that what actually keeps them awake at night is, not being able to find good people to hire.

Power of Visualization

When you start something you are starting a journey. Some people visualize how their journey will look, and some only see what is in front of them. This happens in business too. Some business owners are visionaries, visualizing how their businesses will look years in the future, and some can see no further than the next day.

It is rare to hear about visualization in business, but it is common to hear about it in sports. You hear about it in sports, because coaches and athletes know the power of visualization. They know it works. I played college football, and in addition to spending time conditioning, practicing, studying film, and weightlifting, we also spent time visualizing. The coaches had us close our eyes and visualize executing a perfect tackle or throwing a perfect pass.

If you listen to a post-game interview after a big game, you may hear a football player say they visualized scoring the game-winning touchdown in the Super Bowl or a basketball players say they saw themselves scoring the winning basket in the NBA Finals. They do not replay these scenarios in their minds only once: They replay them over-and-over.

What Is Ahead?

Now that you have compared your expectations to your experiences, what do you visualize going forward? What does your vision look like? Do you see your business accomplishing great things? Are you visualizing at all?

Your vision does not come quietly at night. You construct it. How will you construct your vision going forward?

Chapter 9

Easy Math: Path to Profit

It is common for a small-business owner to rush their product or service to the market without knowing how many units they need to sell or how much of their service they need to provide to earn a profit, assuming that if they make sales, they will be successful. This is not a wise strategy.

There is an easy way to figure out how much business you need to do to earn a profit. Whether you are good at math or not (I am not), and no matter what kind of business you own, there are two simple calculations that will show how much business you need to do.

Breaking Even

Your business breaks even when revenue equals expenses. There are two types of expenses: fixed and variable. Fixed expenses (e.g., rent for office space) are the same regardless of the amount of sales you have, and variable expenses (e.g., utilities) vary, increasing as sales increase and decreasing as sales decrease.

To find your break-even point, add fixed and variable expenses for the month; and do not overlook an expense because it does not seem like much—include everything.

Here is a partial list of expenses: administrative costs, background checks, bank fees, computer hardware and software, drug tests, equipment, food, fuel, insurance, inventory, leases, licenses, maintenance/repairs, payroll, rent, sales commissions, shipping and packaging, supplies, utilities. (Even though you are the owner, you should earn a salary too, an actual check like everyone else with deductions for taxes and FICA.)

After determining monthly expenses, multiply this number by 12 to find your annual expenses. This point bears repeating: Include *every* expense. If you buy water and snacks for the office, include it. Spending $10 per week does not seem like much, but over the course of a year, you will spend $500 on water and snacks!

Where is the Profit?

Now that you know your annual expenses, add to it the amount you want to earn for the year (i.e. your profit) then divide this number by the number of days you intend to work.

If you will work every day except Easter, Thanksgiving, and Christmas, you will work 362 days; so divide this number by 362. If you will work 5 days per week, divide this number by 261 (if you will work 5 days per week and take federal holidays off, you will work 251 days).

The number you are left with shows how much you need to make every single day in order to earn the profit you desire.

Your Numbers

Your break-even number and your profit number are the most important numbers you have—write them down! These are your daily goals. You should see them every day, and you should hit them each day.

If you fall short of your break-even number for the week, for example, to get back on track, you have to exceed your break-even number the next week by the same amount you fell short. If you need weekly sales of $1,000 to break-even, but only had sales of $700, to get back on schedule, your sales should be $1,300 the next week.

Conclusion

You are in business to make a profit, so by calculating your profit number, you will ensure you are on track to do that. By following these numbers, there is no guesswork. You will not have to wait until the end of the year or the end of the quarter—or even the end of the month—to know how your business is performing. You will know at the end of each day.

Chapter 10

Are You Moving Too Fast?

When I used to watch long-distance races on TV, I used to wonder why some runners let other runners get a big lead. I wondered this until I started running half-marathons. What I discovered was, in order to run my best race, I should not concern myself with keeping pace with the other runners. Instead, I should focus on running as fast as I comfortably can.

Before I learned this lesson, because I am competitive, I would try to keep pace with the runners in the lead. I did not realize I was not as well-conditioned as these runners, so when fatigue set-in—and it always did—I would slow down, and runners who *had* been running at their pace would pass me; thus, I would finish at or near the back of the field.

You Set Your Pace

What does running have to do with running a business? Plenty! Whether you are running a business or running a race, you perform best when you perform at a comfortable pace. Also, only you know what pace is comfortable for you.

Some people will tell you are slow and that if you work faster, you will sell more products or services and make more money. They are right! You *will* make more if you sell more, but there is a danger in going too fast. I have trained hundreds of small-business owners from across the country. What I have noticed is, when a small-business owner tries to speed up too much and work at a faster pace than they are comfortable with, they tend to lose control of their business.

Be Comfortable

Going at your pace means working at a speed you are comfortable with, but it also means doing things you are comfortable doing. Here is a not-so-obvious way to move too fast.

A salesperson convinces you that your business *has* to have the new accounting software. All of your competitors are using it! In addition, you have been doing your accounting by hand, and you have made a few mistakes, so the salesperson assures you, you will have no more accounting errors. It will also require less time and effort.

Increased effectiveness and efficiency in less time—how can you refuse! If all of that is not enough, buying this software also allows you to keep pace with your competitors. Therefore, you buy it and install it, but there is one small problem: You have no idea how to use it. You either try to use it, spending more time than before and making more mistakes than before, or you do not use it at all. Knowing you did not need it and really could not afford it.

Speed IS Important

By going slower than your competitors, you *will* miss opportunities, because competitors will get to prospective customers before you, and while success is not completely reliant on speed, speed is a factor. When pursuing a prospective customer, if a competitor arrives before you, they will get first consideration. No matter how good your product or service—even if it is the industry's best—the prospective customer may like what you are offering, but it will mean little if they have already signed a contract with your competitor.

If you begin hearing "Had you been here a week earlier …" over-and-over, it will motivate you to quicken your pace. This reminds me of a slow-moving character Tim Conway played on *The Carol Burnett Show*. Do not move too fast, but do not shuffle along like Mr. Tudball.

In the training classes I teach, some small-business owners were doing things at a relatively fast pace while others were doing them at a relatively slow pace, but what I found funny was, some of the slower-moving owners wondered why their faster-moving peers were having more luck. However, I told them their faster-moving peers were completing ten steps in two days while they were completing them in two weeks, so they should not expect the same results.

It is important that while some of their real-world competitors will move faster, what is most important is, going as fast as they are comfortable going, not as fast as their peers.

Having Too Much

Some small-business owners fail, because they did not have something they needed. Some fail, because they had something they did not know how to use or something they did not need. Here is an example:

Assume you own a restaurant and your food is excellent—people come from neighboring counties for it. Your friend tells you since so many of your customers come from the south side of town, you should open a second restaurant there. Sounds like a good idea.

This seems to be a common problem in the restaurant industry: expanding too soon. This may sound like a good idea, but before expanding, you should ensure your management structure is in place at your initial location and that you have permanent staff.

Similarly, someone may tell you that if you have been in business a certain number of months, you should have a certain number of customers. This line of reasoning fails to consider that, if you had that number of customers, you might drown from too much business! In addition, someone may try to convince you that you need to hire ten or fifteen people, not knowing you are only capable of managing four or five.

Conclusion

When others are ahead of you—even if they are way ahead—do not try to catch them if it means running at a faster pace than you are comfortable with. They may be in better shape and capable of sustaining that pace. Do not concern yourself with them. Run as fast as you comfortably can, and whether you overtake the leaders or not, you *will* finish the race.

Marvin Carolina Jr.

Chapter 11

You Are In A Race!

In 2014, Dennis Kimetto of Kenya set a world record: He ran the Berlin Marathon in 2 hours, 2 minutes, and 57 seconds. Unless you are a distance-running enthusiast, you probably do not know just how fast this is. Trust me: It is *blazing*.

According to the U.S. Army Physical Fitness Guide, to be in the top 1% of their age group, a 17- to 21-year-old runner would have to run 1 mile in 6 minutes and 30 seconds. That is a fairly-fast pace. Dennis Kimetto's average mile was run in 4 minutes and 41 seconds, and he sustained that blistering pace for 26 miles!

I have discussed speed in a previous article ("Are You Moving Too Fast?"), but I am discussing it again, because it is crucial that you understand its importance. From what I have observed, most small-business owners do not understand its importance, because far too many of them conduct business at a leisurely pace, which tells me they have no idea that they are in a race.

An Amazing Race

I watch *The Amazing Race* every week. It is one of my favorite shows, because it is exciting and because it is a lot like business. Each team is comprised of two people, and the eleven teams have to complete a series of tasks, which take them around the world. The team that completes all of the tasks and reaches the finish line first, wins.

Each day brings a different task, and the team completing that day's task first gets to start first the next day. If a team completes a task but does not complete it correctly, they have to start over and cannot move-on until the task is completed correctly.

To succeed, each participant has to be resourceful and communicate well, but the key to succeeding in this race—and in business—is working quickly. Everything is done quickly.

Your Amazing Race

Children do things quickly. When I was young, my parents were always telling me to slow down. "Do not run in the house!" "Do not eat so fast!" This was good advice then, but when I launched my small-business many years ago, I realized doing things quickly was an asset.

You are now all grown up and a business owner; therefore, I can say this to you: Do not listen to your parents! In business, the faster you move, the more you get done and the more sales you will make.

Some business owners are obsessed with completing every task perfectly. I am not suggesting that you work so fast that you produce shoddy work—that is a recipe for failure. What I am suggesting is, getting each task right, but also remember you are in a race, so work quickly.

A Pit Stop

Speed is obviously important in auto racing, but a casual viewer might not realize some of the most exciting—and pivotal—moments in a race often occur in the pits.

When a driver needs fuel, new tires, or an adjustment to their car, they make a pit stop. The pit crew has to complete the task and complete it quickly. If the crew fails to do its job correctly, their driver will not have a chance of winning. Their driver could get hurt or worse.

If the crew fails to do its job quickly, their driver will lose valuable time. Each crew performs identical tasks and the crews that perform the tasks the quickest give their drivers competitive advantage. The one- or two-second advantage gained in the pit is often the difference between winning and finishing second.

Do Not Overdo It

I teach small-business owners across the country, and have noticed that most of them approach a task with the intention of completing it perfectly every time; thus, giving no thought to how long it will take. As previously stated, you should do everything to the best of your ability, because quality is the most-important consideration, but it is not the only consideration.

Assume you are scheduling a meeting with a prospective customer. You do your homework—researching their product or service, market, competitors, reading their customer reviews, and visiting their website—but you want to find an interesting fact or anecdote that will make yourself stand-out, so to give yourself extra time, you schedule the meeting for Tuesday instead of Monday. You are about to leave your office on Tuesday morning to meet the prospective customer, and you are confident, because you are thoroughly prepared, and your sales pitch is sharp. Then you get a call. It is the prospective customer. They want to cancel. Why? They met with one of your competitors on Monday and agreed to do business with them.

Conclusion

Running a business is like running a marathon: It is a *long* way to the finish line, but do not be fooled into thinking you can jog the race and still be competitive. You cannot. The runners whizzing by you will outperform you in the race, and the business owners whizzing by you will outperform you in the market.

Marvin Carolina Jr.

Chapter 12

Insurance Is the Biggest Waste of Money ... Until You Need It

As far back as I can remember, my father was in the insurance business. I remember him telling my mother on many occasions how happy people were when he did bring them their claims checks. Some of them, he said, even cried. As a kid I knew that having insurance was a good thing, but it was not until I was older that I understood why.

I launched my beverage business in 1992, and like most small-business owners, I had a tight budget. Using a delivery truck, I was required to carry commercial insurance. Business grew; therefore, I hired an employee to make my deliveries, and I knew my employee was a good driver, but odds were he would eventually be involved in an accident, so I was not at all surprised when he called and said someone had run into him.

My insurance agent informed me that I was covered—they would pay for everything. Having insurance was definitely a good thing and now I knew why. I could not afford to repair my truck, and it would have been nearly impossible to find the money to rent a truck. Without my insurance, the accident might have driven me out of business.

What It Is

You can buy insurance to protect your business from lots of potentially-catastrophic events, but when you get down to it, an insurance policy simply says that in exchange for you paying a monthly or quarterly premium, your insurance company will pay you if your business suffers an economic loss. If, for example, a June tornado were to drop an elm or oak tree on top of your business causing thousands of dollars of damage, your insurance would pay for the damage.

Why You Need It

If you have never filed an insurance claim, each time you pay your premium you may wonder if paying insurance is a waste of money. I assure you: If you are in business long enough, you *will* see the value of insurance.

What would happen to your business if a key employee left? If someone slipped and fell on your business' premises? Few small-business owners actually budget for something like this to happen, but by paying premiums, that is essentially what you are doing. In addition, insurance protects you from an act of God, but it also protects you from more-likely financial burdens.

A 2013, a CNBC study found that the leading cause of personal bankruptcy was unpaid medical bills—not credit-card bills or unpaid mortgages. Being liable for a huge medical bill after you have been rushed to the emergency room or have undergone a costly medical procedure puts enormous financial burden on an individual. In the same way, being liable for a huge business judgment puts enormous financial burden on a small business.

Have Employees?

If you have employees you are required to carry worker's compensation insurance and unemployment insurance, but you probably will not need disability insurance. Unless you have employees in California, Hawaii, New Jersey, New York, Puerto Rico, or Rhode Island, you do not need disability insurance. Some employers in those states carry disability insurance to make their benefits more attractive and their businesses more competitive.

I know small-business owners who have landed employees simply, because they (owners) offered health insurance. Health insurance is especially attractive to older workers, and many of them say health insurance is more important to them than income—some will even accept a low wage simply to get insurance.

This is a win-win: The small business gets a skillful, seasoned employee without having to pay top dollar. The employee gets medical insurance, assuring that if they incur a costly medical bill, their insurance will cover most or all of the bill.

Limit Liability

If your business is a sole proprietorship or a partnership, you would be personally liable for your business' debts and legal judgements. In addition, if your business was sued, your liability could exceed your annual sales—it *could* exceed the value of your business!

Many business owners form limited liability companies (LLC's), as the name suggests, which your legal liability would not exceed the value of your business. In other words, though you could lose your business, you would not lose your house or your car or any other non-business asset.

I know what it is like managing a tight budget; therefore, I am not suggesting you buy every type of business insurance imaginable, but I am suggesting you carry liability insurance (in addition to what is legally required). It is a game-changer! When something unforeseen happens—and it will—getting a claim check from your agent may also bring you to tears.

Chapter 13

Job Well Done

When I sat down to write this book, which is specifically for small-business owners, I put myself in your shoes. This is easy to do, because for five years I *was* in your shoes. I owned my own business, in Atlanta, and the things I talk about in my book are lessons I learned by trial-and-error.

I enjoy writing, because it allows me to share lessons learned. I will not be talking about profit margins or technology nor ways to make your business more effective and more efficient. Instead of offering something new, I will be acknowledging several things I should have acknowledged long ago.

You Are Still Here

First, let me say this: "Congratulations—you are still in business!" I mean this sincerely. No matter how your business is performing—whether you are the industry leader or not—and whether you have been in business two years or twenty, I applaud you.

Whatever improvements need to be made to allow you to realize your business' potential, you still have time to make them. According to the quote, "Eighty percent of success is showing up." You are still in the game, so in my opinion, that makes you successful.

It *Is* Difficult

Second, I want to acknowledge that being a small-business owner is *enormously* difficult and I personally know that! Everyone looks to you for answers, guidance leadership and results. That is a lot of pressure. Pressure creates stress, and stress drains you emotionally, mentally *and* physically. Not only that, you are not the only one who deals with the stress small-business ownership brings. Your family deals with it too.

If the tone of my book suggests I think it is easy to implement the things I recommend, I apologize. Many of the things discussed are somewhat difficult to implement, and some of them are also time-consuming and costly.

In one area I am asking you to be an expert accountant, in another an IT whiz, in another a marketing and sales genius, and in still another an expert at identifying talent and the shrewdness to bring talented individuals into your business at a reasonable salary. None of these are easy to do -- I know that.

Why I Do It

If I seem to be force-feeding you through a water hose, it is only, because I understand business ownership, and know what needs to happen to build a successful business. I teach small-businesses across the country how to run profitable businesses, and though I may seem forceful at times, I am only trying to help. If you know me—and many of you do—you know I have good intention, but need to say it from time-to-time.

Conclusion

As a small-business owner, you are thrilled when you land a big contract or sign a big client. You have so much to do, that you cannot enjoy it for long, because you have to get back to work. It is like scoring a touchdown.

You are happy you finally made it to the end zone, and you are proud of yourself, but when you look up at the scoreboard and see you are down four touchdowns, the touchdown is not quite as sweet.

You have so much left to do, but you are making progress. You are doing—and have done—an exceptional job! If you ever feel I am giving you a hard time, remind yourself that it is, because I know what it takes to get where you are trying to go. Remind yourself, that I am doing it because I care.

Chapter 14

Social Skills: Still on Top

We live in the Digital Age where we primarily communicate with computers and mobile devices. Instead of meeting in-person, we Skype. Instead of calling, we e-mail or text. Society increasingly relies on social media to communicate, and as a business owner, you should too.

You should have a website, but you should also connect with and market to the public. Facebook, YouTube, Twitter, LinkedIn—use them to keep your business and your brand in front of people. Social media appears to have taken over, it is still important to connect with people in a personal way. A firm handshake, a sincere smile, and a pleasant personality will grow your business faster than anything else.

Lasting Impressions

Having good social skills is more than merely speaking well. It is more than working the room and meeting people with ease. Having good social skills boils down to this: Do people like you and trust you?

Assume you meet with a prospective client, but they get the impression you are arrogant and condescending. Even if they like your product or service, do you think you will get their business? You may think a business owner will surely do what is best for their bottom line regardless of someone's personality; but I disagree, so does Daniel Kahneman.

Daniel Kahneman is a Nobel Prize-winning psychologist who found that people would rather do business with a person they like and trust than with someone they do not like or trust—even if the likeable person is offering a lower-quality product or service at a higher price!

More Important Than Everything Else

With so much competition in the market, it is important you show how your business is different from the others. Doing something exceptionally well obviously makes your business unique, and it presents a compelling competitive advantage. Perhaps you have the best product or service. In addition, your business has the lowest prices and it is the most innovative.

Any of these reasons will give you a competitive advantage that will be difficult for your competitors to overcome, but if you have outstanding social skills, these skills alone will cause your business to grow faster than anything else.

Not Just Customers

You do not merely communicate with clients and prospective clients; you also communicate with advisors, your business partner, employees, mentors, and vendors. These communications are also important.

When your business is facing a crisis, for example, and you convene your staff to explain your strategy for overcoming the crisis, how is your voice? Is it full and firm, inspiring your staff to rally around you or is it weak and unsure? If it is the latter, you may say the right things, but they will not believe you, because your non-verbal cues are sending a different message.

What about your vendors—do you talk to them? If you do and have built a rapport, they will bring ideas about how you can save money or market better. Any number of suggestions could be submitted to you that you would not have received unless you built a rapport with them.

How Good Are Yours?

Take an honest look at your social skills, and assess how good they are. If they are poor, you have two options:

improve them or find someone in your business to fill-in for you when good social skills are needed.

If you do not know how good your social skills are—and I recommend you find out. Ask people who will give you honest answers. Ask them to describe how you come across, and listen to what they say. If someone gives you an answer you do not like, do not ask the same question in a different way hoping to get the answer you want. Accept it.

Conclusion

You are the face of your business, and whether you are a charismatic extrovert or a reclusive introvert, your personality impacts your bottom line. Technology continues to advance, but as long as there are people running businesses and making decisions, social skills will never become obsolete. Business will continue to get more competitive, but as Jeffrey Gitomer wrote in *The Little Red Book of Selling*, "All else being equal, people do business with people they like."

Chapter 15

Stand Out in a Crowded Market

No matter what product or service your business provides, you have competitors in a market that is as crowded as ever; therefore, your business *has* to stand out. Some business owners agree with the adage "there's no such thing as bad publicity," and they look for unusual—and in some cases, bizarre—ways of drawing attention to their business. What usually works better, though, is finding positive, original ways of getting attention.

I have studied small-business owners for years and have found these methods work best:

Be Fast

If the price and quality of your product or service is comparable to the competitions', one of the easiest ways to stand out is being faster. Meeting with a prospective customer on one day and following-up the very next day will get their attention. They will notice, because you followed-up quickly *and* because it took your competitors days to follow-up.

Do not assume being fast allows you to sacrifice quality. It does not. Today's customers want quality and they want it fast, so when they e-mail you or leave you a message, they expect a prompt—and accurate—reply. If they have a problem today, they want it resolved today, which is why some companies offer same-day service.

Speed is also important for another reason. Assume you meet with a prospective customer on Thursday, but instead of following-up the next day, you convince yourself you can follow-up on Monday. After all, you have other work to do, so they surely will not expect you to follow-up the next day; and since your competitors' businesses are closed over the weekend, getting back in touch with them on Monday seems like a good idea.

A lot can happen in a day—let alone several days. The prospective customer was excited after your meeting, but after you allowed a few days to pass, their excitement waned. When you call them on Monday and do not hear the enthusiasm you heard on Thursday, you will know you let too much time pass.

Impress

Most businesses give consumers what they want and no more: "You asked for a widget, and I provided you a widget." There is nothing extraordinary about that, but if you meet with a prospective customer and promise to follow-up in a few days, but follow up the next day. You have exceeded their expectations.

If your business merely does what is expected, it will blend in—not stand out. Give your customers and prospective customers more than they expect. Wow them! Learn about your customers' businesses and their industries so that you understand the challenges they face. When you meet with them, be prepared and anticipate what questions they might ask.

Do more than is expected in any way you can, and your business will stand out.

Innovate

I cannot overstate the importance of creativity and innovation: of all the ways of making your business stand out, innovating is the best way. It is the essence of entrepreneurship. Offer something the market has never seen before—in this ever-changing world where everything is new—and people *will* notice.

Some people mistakenly assume that to come up with an innovative idea, they have to create something new. Not true. Some innovations are simply new ways of providing old products or services.

Uber is an entrepreneurial venture, but what is Uber really? A taxi service! Its founders were not struck with a bolt of inspiration: they had trouble getting a cab one snowy night in Paris, and they thought how great it would be if people could get a cab with the press of a button. They simply saw how technology could be added to an existing service to solve their problem.

Innovations do not become popular, because they are new; they become popular, because they make our lives easier. While it is easy to marvel at the technology that makes an innovation possible, remember this: Innovation is about convenience, not technology. Uber allows you to hail a cab using your mobile device. Amazon was created to allow consumers to buy books without having to drive to a bookstore.

Examine the ways you interact with customers and prospective customers, and ask yourself—and them—what you can do to make their lives easier.

Conclusion

If your business wows consumers, works quickly, or introduces innovative ways of doing things, it *will* stand out. If it consistently does all three, it will be an industry leader. There is one more step. When your business does something exceptionally well, let the world know. What good is a competitive advantage if no one knows about it?

Chapter 16

Strategy vs. Tactics

In business, strategy and tactics have very different meanings. *Strategy* is the plan that lists your goals, and you have an overarching (primary) business strategy and strategies for each area of your business. Your strategy has goals, and you have a short-term strategy and a long-term strategy. One of your marketing strategies, for example, may be to have a presence on social networks.

Tactics are activities undertaken to ensure you accomplish your strategic goals. Staying with this example, one of your marketing tactics may be using Facebook, LinkedIn, and Twitter and creating a blog, in addition to maintaining your business website.

Strategic Plan

Your strategic plan keeps you on track and shows which activities you should spend time on. There are lots of things you can do during the workday, but by keeping your strategic goals in mind, you will know which activities will help you realize your goals. Your strategic plan answers questions like these:

- What are my sales goals?
- What are my long-term profit-margin goals?
- What do I want to do next month? Next year?
- What resources will I need next month? Next year?

Wandering Aimlessly

Lots of small-business owners embark on their business journey without taking time to plan their trip, launching their business while giving no thought to where they want their business to go. They have no idea where they are headed. They are simply hoping to run into someone who wants their product or service.

One or the Other

Some small-business owners have a strategic plan, but have no boots on the ground to connect their activities to their strategy. Some owners are full of ideas about how to make their business profitable, but they have no plans, goals, or objectives; so even though they are making sales, their business is not progressing.

The second owner is more common than the first. Lots of owners stay busy with activities they think are helping their business, and while they can keep their business alive using this method, it probably will not survive for long—and it will not come close to realizing its potential.

Finally, there are owners who have a strategy and tactics, but fail to use them. These owners keep busy with activities designed to help them accomplish their strategic goal, but while they have a strategic plan, they do not use it. It collects dust on the shelf, because they have not looked at it in months or longer.

Sales Strategy

If your sales strategy is trying to make a sale whenever you come across someone interested in your product or service, you do not have a sales strategy. You do have a sales strategy; however, if you can answer questions like these:

- What is my sales goal?
- Which customers am I pursuing?
- Which customers do I enjoy working with?
- Which customers provide the biggest profit margin?

Not a Business Plan

Your strategic plan can be part of your business plan, but the two are not the same. You typically create a business plan to apply for a loan from a bank. Your business plan explains, among other things, how your business operates, who your competitors are, and what competitive advantage(s) you enjoy.

Your strategic plan identifies your overarching goal and your area-specific goals (e.g., marketing, sales). It guides your activities, so at the start of each day, you know your expected outcomes and your expected income.

Conclusion

It is usually best to plan before you act—in business and in life—so it is no surprise you need strategy *and* tactics, working together as a cohesive unit, to run a successful business. One last thing: Write down your strategy and your tactics. You will forget them if you do not and if your strategic plan is dusty, it is time for the two of you to get reacquainted.

Chapter 17

This Is Not Working

Winston Churchill, known for quotes about politics, war, and leadership, has a little-known quote every business owner should heed: "To improve is to change, so to be perfect is to have changed often." I am not suggesting you'll arrive at perfection, but I am suggesting that by being willing to change, you will ensure your small business fulfills its potential.

Think about your product or service—is it the same as it was when you launched your business? If it is, and you justify having made no improvements by saying your customers are still buying it, so they must be happy with it, you are running the risk of losing some of your customers to a competitor who *will* upgrade their product or service.

If this does happen, when their new-and-improved version hits the market, do not get mad. You may laugh it off by saying you could have made the same improvements, and this may be true, but you did not! If this happens you *should* get mad, mad at yourself for not offering your customers a better product or service.

Sequence

Every single thing in your business needs to be improved. Not just your product or service. Every policy, procedure, and process. Before you can improve them, you must review them, so be sure your review includes each step:

1. Identify all the parts that need to be reviewed.
2. Determine the goal.
3. Determine how often to conduct the review.

What The Public Sees

You want to improve your product or service, but you also want to improve every direct and indirect message each department sends: advertising, customer service, marketing, public relations, and sales. You have an overarching message you want to send (i.e., your brand), so ensure every activity and message from every employee in every department works together to send that overarching message. Again and again.

What The Public Does Not See

The public knows about your product or service, and they form an opinion about your business according to how professional, friendly, and knowledgeable your employees are; however, the public has no idea if your policies, procedures, and processes are effective and efficient and they do not want to know! You should know how well they are working.

Do not be so consumed with producing the best product or service in the market that you give no thought to how efficiently you produce your product or offer your service. If a competitor gets a better wholesale price from a manufacturer than they were once getting, allowing them to lower their price, even though their product is inferior to yours, they are going to steal some of your customers. Be on the lookout for ways to conduct business more effectively and more efficiently, because I assure you, your competitors are.

Nothing Is Off-Limits

It bears repeating: Everything needs to be reviewed, from the answering-machine greeting the public hears to the price you charge for your product or service. I occasionally use a sports analogy to illustrate a point, and this one came to mind.

College and professional football teams have an army of coaches. There is one head coach, and he has a staff of assistant coaches. Each assistant coach is responsible for a group of players according to their position (e.g., quarterbacks, running backs, defensive backs), and each assistant coach not only knows each of his position players, he knows them well.

Most football players are superstitious—I know, because I played football at Georgia Tech—and among football players, field-goal kickers are the most superstitious. Here is the scenario:

The assistant coach responsible for the kickers knows the field-goal kicker's lucky socks were not shipped with the team's uniforms, and he also noticed in pre-game warm-ups that his kicker missed several routine kicks he normally makes.

A pair of socks seems trivial, but if the head coach has to decide whether or not to use the kicker in a crucial situation, could not this information—which could determine the game's outcome—prove important?

How Often?

How often do you conduct employee performance evaluations? Probably annually, and that is fine, but how often do you review your policies, procedures, and processes? Annually, bi-annually, quarterly? If you are like most small-business owners your answer is, "When something happens that forces me to review them." If you are like most small-business owners, you are reviewing them much too late.

It is up to you to determine how often you will review them, but each policy, procedure, and process should have a review schedule. Some can be reviewed more often than others, but you should always look for ways to improve each of them.

Expectations

In addition to having a review date, each process should have two things: an expectation (i.e., a goal) and an end date. Assume you have e-mailed letters of introduction to prospective customers, but you are changing your approach, and now you will be cold-calling prospective customers. Before sending your first e-mail, determine how many new customers you intend to make (i.e., your goal) and by what date (i.e., your time limit).

This allows you to identify what is performing on par, what is performing exceptionally well, and what is performing poorly.

Conclusion

Every activity your business engages in, whether externally or internally, consumes time and money. To fulfill your business' potential, you should upgrade your product or service, and also improve every policy, procedure, and process by finding more effective and more efficient ways of providing what you sell.

Marvin Carolina Jr.

Chapter 18

Who Monitors Your Technology?

In today's ultra-competitive, technology-driven market, to grow your business, you should use technology. The more you use, the better. I have written two articles about technology, which demonstrates how important I think it is, but I have to back-track just a bit.

While technology makes your job easier and makes your employees and your business more effective and efficient, you cannot simply install it and forget about it. You have to understand what it is producing. Here is an example:

Assume you are poring over your business' financial spreadsheets, because you have a decision to make, and your technology is producing numbers like 40 or 50—numbers that are out-of-the-ordinary—when it should be producing numbers like 10 or 15. If you did not know what numbers *should* be produced, you would accept that was being produced and make your decision based on inaccurate information.

Perhaps the technology was fine. There could have been an input error or an error in the formula you used. No matter where the problem was, if you knew what numbers to expect, you would have known the numbers produced were inaccurate.

GPS

I have lived in Kansas City for 15 years, and while I use GPS often, I do not enter an address in it and blindly follow its directions. When I enter an address in GPS, it always sends me through town. Why? Going through town is the shortest route, but it is not the fastest route: I may have to stop at ten lights! Therefore, I almost always take the highway. My trips are a mile or two longer, but I always arrive sooner than I would have if I had gone through town.

Auto Correct

I am not the best speller, so when I am typing an e-mail, I rely on auto-correct to catch my mistakes. Sometimes, it changes a word I have typed or it capitalizes a word I do not want capitalized; therefore, before I send what I have typed, I review it.

Auto-correct is invaluable if you are not a great speller, but if you blindly rely on it—and I know people who do, so I am saying this from experience—it will embarrass you. You do not want to send something offensive, especially in a professional letter or e-mail.

Calling an Audible

If you watch football, you know teams use state-of-the art technology to get every competitive advantage. However, for all the money they spend, teams rely on their players to make the final decisions.

Here is how an offensive play is run. The head coach or offensive coordinator calls the play, which the quarterback hears in his helmet. Since neither the coach nor the coordinator know what alignment the defense will be in, the quarterback has to determine what alignment the defense is in and determine if the play he is been given will work. If he does not think it will, he changes it.

For all of the computer-generated tendency charts that predict what alignment the defense will likely be in, the quarterback makes the final determination, so if the defense lines up in an unexpected way, it is his responsibility to change the play.

Too Much Is Bad Too

I get frustrated when a business owner says they are too busy to learn technology. I understand they have a lot to do, but what they fail to realize is, if they use the technology, they will have *more* free time and it will make their business more efficient! I get even more frustrated, when a business owner installs technology and trusts it without question.

Technology certainly gives your business a competitive advantage, but no matter how advanced it is, it is not foolproof. You *must* monitor it. When technology makes a mistake—and it will—or when it produces something inaccurate, you will catch it. If you do not monitor it, then you will not, catch it and it might result in you making a bad business decision.

Conclusion

Do not fool yourself into thinking you can continue doing business the way you have always done it and be successful. You cannot. The most-successful business owners ensure their businesses are equipped with cutting-edge technology, but I have talked to enough of them to know, they monitor their cutting-edge technology closely. Which is why you should monitor yours.

Chapter 19

Hire A Business Consultant … For Free

What do Bill Gates, Steve Jobs, Oprah Winfrey, and Mark Zuckerberg have in common? Each has been extraordinarily successful and each had a mentor. Whether you call them a Business Consultant, a Coach, or a Mentor, you need one. Running a business is difficult. You are more likely to be successful if you have someone to rely on for advice.

What They Do

A Consultant advises you how to run your business. Since there are hundreds of things that demand your attention, you do not have time to consider them all. When you want to know if your existing process is customer-friendly and efficient, for example, ask your Consultant.

Why You Need One

Your business may be the most important thing in the world to you, and you spend long hours every day staying on top of things, but you still miss important details. Did you know your Receptionist uses the office phone to make personal calls or that your website is difficult to understand?

A Consultant helps in lots of ways:

- **Advice:** Reading business books and taking business classes are fine, but they are more helpful when you can ask questions of someone who knows *your* business.
- **Cool Head:** You have invested your entire savings into your business. It *has* to succeed. This stress, clouds judgment and often leads to you making unwise business decisions. Your Consultant is not stressed: they have nothing to lose.
- **Encouragement:** At times, you may wonder if starting your business was a good idea, but you do not discuss it with your spouse. You do not want to worry them. Your Consultant reminds you of what you have accomplished and what you have overcome. They will not just say, "Things will be fine": they will help you make things fine.
- **Improve Skills:** Unlike a book or a class, your Consultant knows you. They know what you do

well, but more importantly, they know what you may not: what you *do not* do well. They will help you strengthen weak areas, so you become a better employer and a better businessperson.

- **New Ideas:** You may be brilliant, and you may have excelled in Ivy League business school, but you do not have a monopoly on good ideas. Your Consultant, with their unique experiences and opinions, will think of things you had not considered.
- **NOT Like-Minded:** Do not limit yourself to finding a Consultant who thinks like you. You want a Consultant with a different background. In fact, having a Consultant who sees things exactly as you see them is a waste of time: what good is having two people who see things the same way?
- **Perspective:** You are busy with tasks that must be completed, so you miss important details. Your Consultant has a broader perspective, so they will see things you miss. In addition, they will see how your business looks to your customer.
- **Venting:** Sometimes you need to yell and you should. However, yell in front of your employees, and they may question your ability to lead or they may question your sanity. Yell in front of your spouse, and they may worry you do not know what you are doing. Your Consultant will not

have these concerns and after you have calmed down, they will help you find solutions.

Got To Listen

Your $300-per-hour Consultant, with their MBA from a Top Ten business school is of no benefit to you if you are not willing to listen to their recommendations. If you close your ears thinking "No one knows my business better than me," you will not be in business long.

I Listened ... Now What?

You listened to your Consultant. Congratulations! You are exactly *halfway* to the finish line. If you want your business to succeed and grow, you will take the all-important next step: doing what your Consultant recommends.

Whether in a formal presentation with your MBA Consultant or in the basement with your brother-in-law, regardless of who came up with the recommendations, if you do not implement them, they mean absolutely nothing.

How Much?

If hiring a Consultant is best for you and your business that is what you should do. They are not cheap (fees start at $150-per-hour), but hire the right Consultant, and you will be glad you did.

You do not *have* to hire a Consultant: you can get valuable input from a friend or relative. You can have one Consultant or several (like me), and you can get one before going into business or after you have been in business. There is no bad time to get good advice.

All it costs to have a Consultant is a little consideration. Meet when and where it is convenient for them: better that you drive across town than have them drive across town. Meet over lunch or dinner ... and be sure to pick-up the tab!

Are They Credible?

If your Consultant does not have a computer background, do not ask them how to upgrade your business' operating system to Microsoft Vista. In other words, if you need specialized advice, ask someone with specialized education and training.

If you are a caterer, you do not need specialized advice. Consultants are great at spotting resources we are not using. They may suggest, rather than you delivering the food, you hire someone to deliver it. You will pay them less than your hourly wage, freeing you to cook more food and operate more efficiently.

Why Does Everyone Not Have One?

Perhaps you think you can run your business without help. Actually, you can. However, you will run it better—*much* better—with help. It is no coincidence some of the smartest, most-successful business owners found mentors, and it is not surprising the vast majority of business owners say having a mentor is one of the reasons their business has thrived. What *is* surprising, is that more business owners, with so much at stake, do not have them. What about you?

Chapter 20

Failing in Good Times

To survive and grow in business requires that you endure the upswings and downturns of the economy. While the Great Recession is well behind us, it claimed lots of victims: according to the *Business Journals*, during just the first two years of the Great Recession (which began in December 2007), 170,000 small businesses failed.

What I find odd about some small-business failures is, though they struggle during tough economic times like everyone else, they survive. Only to go out-of-business when the economy gets stronger.

Why Now?

Logic suggests a business would fail during an economic downturn when demand and sales have drastically reduced; but this is not always the case. What often happens is, in order to survive a recession, a small-business owner is often forced to dip into their cash reserves to meet payroll, cover expenses, and pay costs incurred from producing their product or providing their service.

When the economy improves and demand for their product or service increases, the small-business owner has to spend more to meet increased demand; but having depleted their cash reserves, which they used to get through the recession, they lack the cash needed to meet demand; therefore, they are driven out of business.

Do Not Take Everything

When you are in the midst of a recession, your phone does not ring nearly as often as it once did. It may take days—or weeks—to find even one new client. As the recession comes to an end, the economy picks up, and your phone begins ringing again. You are getting work, perhaps more than you can handle, and you want to grab all the work you can get!

The key to surviving an economic slowdown, is to be strategic (i.e. selective). You will be tempted to get all the work you can, as your competitors are, but resist the temptation.

Think back to before the recession hit: you had high standards. You did not lower them then and should not lower them now. If you are not selective and take every job you can get in a weakened economy, you will find yourself accepting a lot of cheap work, which you will discover is not *good* work.

Cash

Small-business owners should also be selective when accepting jobs in a recovering economy, because they probably lack huge cash reserves—they probably spent the cash they had to stay afloat during the recession.

Cash is obviously important, but even more so during tough economic times. With reduced demand, you have less coming in, so you are often forced to turn to a bank; but it is harder to get cash from a bank during a recession. When you apply for a loan or a line-of-credit, the bank will likely reject your application and say your business performed poorly in recent months. Businesses tend to perform poorly in a recession!

Economic Dashboard

Do you monitor your economic gauges: balance statements, cash-flow statements, income statements? You should. When the economy awakens from an economic slumber and demand for your product or service is robust, as you decide which jobs to accept and which to reject, rely on your gauges. They will indicate which jobs are profitable and which are not.

If you want to run cash through your business and choose cash-flow over profit, for example, reconsider. While this will bring much-needed cash, when you consider net profit, you discover you will actually lose money on this job.

Even if you are desperate for cash and need to accept a job that some of your economic indicators implore you to reject, the indicators that support you taking the job will tell you what you need to do to make money on that job.

Though today's economy is relatively strong, it is never a bad time to read—and heed—your economic indicators. Whether good times or bad, stay focused on your goals, and maintain your high standards. You have them for a reason.

Chapter 21

The Tired Entrepreneur

Do you get enough sleep? If you are like 40% of adults, you do not. What *is* enough sleep? Sleep experts recommend adults get seven to nine hours of sleep each night. Some adults need more. It is important you know how much sleep you need and it is important you get it. If you are not getting enough sleep, you are hurting yourself *and* your business.

A study of college students concluded that the students who got six hours of sleep or less each night performed as poorly as the group of students *who had not slept for 48 hours!*

Without adequate sleep, it is impossible to perform at your best. Here are some symptoms you exhibit when you have not had enough sleep:

- Forgetfulness
- Impatience

- Inability to concentrate
- Inability to focus
- Inability to make good decisions
- Inability to solve problems
- Irritability
- Lack of creativity
- Lack of energy

Lots of adults substitute coffee for a good night's sleep, which is perhaps why caffeine has been called *the* most-popular drug. Caffeine temporarily makes you more alert by blocking sleep-inducing chemicals in your brain and by releasing more adrenaline into your blood. If you drink no more than three eight-ounce cups of coffee each day, there are no health risks, but understand this: caffeine is a poor substitute for sleep.

Caffeine makes you more alert by tricking your brain into thinking you do not need sleep, when you actually do. Caffeine makes you more alert than you would be without it, it does not make you as alert, for example, as you would be if you had gotten a good night's sleep.

It is easy to forgo sleep when you are running a business, because you have to do *everything*. You talk to customers, prospective customers, and unhappy customers. You balance the ledger and make sales pitches and you produce your product or provide your service.

With so much to do, you routinely fall into bed after Midnight and roll out of it before 6:00 a.m. You start each day the way you ended the previous one: tired and stressed. Whether you drink a few cups of coffee or twice that many, you are tired. When you are tired you make bad decisions and bad decisions produce bad results.

Here is my advice: stop working nights and weekends. You think you are getting ahead of the competition by working when they are sleeping, but what you are actually doing is, having a person inferior to you in every way—who is also a poor decision-maker—run your business. Is this *really* the person you want running your business!

You can survive on five- or six-hours of sleep, but for how long? Until you make $100,000 a year in sales? Until you get through tax season? Until your fiscal year ends? A lack of sleep not only keeps you from performing at your best, it also causes health problems:

- Diabetes
- Heart attack
- Heart disease
- Heart failure
- High blood-pressure
- Stroke

Which of your goals is worth even one of these?

Business is competition, and like any competition, there are things you control and things you do not. A football player, for example, controls how hard he works, what he eats, and how much he exercises and sleeps. You control how many hours you work, what you eat, and how much you exercise and sleep.

None of these appear on your balance sheet or income statement, but they are as important as the items that do. You control how many hours you work. Think of it this way: working too much is as bad for business—and in some ways worse—as working too little. You recoil at the thought of working five-hour days, but you would have better health if you did, and you would be more productive.

Whether your business is worth a few thousand dollars or a few million, *you* are its most valuable asset, so it makes good business sense to take care of yourself. Eat right, exercise, and get *plenty* of sleep—you cannot make a better investment.

CONCLUSION

I am excited that you have gained more insights into having the ability to compete in today's business environment is a key to success, as well as, understanding the rules of competition and the impact you have in that playing field. Sometimes competition is viewed as negative, but we compete every day. As I said in my introduction, some people just do it a lot better than others.

If after reading my book you decided to implement one thing, I am pleased. Further, if that one thing had a great impact on you, then my expectation has been met. If you have implemented several things from the insights published in this book - you have exceeded my expectations. Thank you for that!

Please give this book or purchase a new one for someone else, so that it can continue to impact the lives of people in business and community! See you in the next Business Strategy and Execution book! Cool deal!

Marvin Carolina Jr.

About the Author

Marvin Carolina Jr., President and CEO of Team Carolina, a team of business consultants, speakers and development trainers. He is former vice president at JE Dunn Construction, writes business articles specifically for small-business owners. His articles have appeared on the Kansas City Star's online publication (kansascity.com) and in Thinking Bigger magazine. He teaches business owners how to climb the ladder of success—and reach the top!

Marvin, and his programs, has been recognized for his community involvement in Kansas City—Ace Award, Community Champion, Top 40 in Their 40's Business and Community Leader, Top Contractors for Diversity—and across the country: Innovation Award (Houston), Hispanic Community Builder Award (Atlanta).

Marvin earned his Bachelor's degree in Industrial Management from Georgia Tech (Atlanta) and his Master's degree in Community Development from North Park University (Chicago). He lives in Kansas City, Missouri, with his wife and two sons.

Contact Marvin Carolina Jr.:

www.marvincarolina.com

marvin@marvincarolina.com